Ten Commandments against Abuse: Love without War

by

Marsha R. Robinson, PhD

If you are being abused, seek professional help in getting out of your situation. This book is not written by a professional counselor.

To read more about this topic in a book written by a professional authority, see Patricia Evans' *The Verbally Abusive Relationship: How to Recognize It and How to Respond.*

Ten Commandments against Abuse: Love without War

by

Marsha R. Robinson

Copyright 2019 Marsha R. Robinson. All rights reserved.
ISBN 978-0-578-58736-3

Table of Contents

1st Commandment – 1
2nd Commandment – 33
3rd Commandment – 45
4th Commandment – 51
5th Commandment – 61
6th Commandment – 71
7th Commandment – 83
8th Commandment – 91
9th Commandment – 95
10th Commandment – 107
Conclusion – 113

*****

Chapter 1
The First Commandment

I am the Lord your God, who brought you out of the land of Egypt, out of the house of slavery. You shall have no other gods before Me.

Let us pray.
Creator God, whose love of the universe is evident in the detailed spaces between parts of atoms and in the beauty of galaxies far away, we know that You pay attention to the details in our lives and in the lives of those around us. By reading this book, we enter into a community of humans who are anxious about domestic violence, ordinary violence, and violence committed as acts of political and interpersonal warfare. So much is good in the universe and in so-

Ten Commandments against Abuse: Love without War

ciety. So much is not good and this brings us together in this moment. May this attempt to explore the Ten Commandments, as Jesus modeled for us in the few surviving lessons we have, be a productive one that inspires us to bring more love into the lives of those living in a daily state of war. May we find ways in which to live a beautiful, loving life. So be it.

In the dark hours of a winter night in my early childhood, I remember my father and mother bundling me into the car to drive to the home of a very old man who was trying to beat his very old wife to death. Again. I remember my father saying to my mother how tired he was of rushing over to stop this old man and how often he talked to him. That old man was the type of man who kept his wife at home in a small, frame house that he built, a house with no indoor toilet and no running hot water in the middle of a city of more than 500,000 people where thousands of people still used outhouses in 1970. So, that was not strange.

The old man built a two-storied colonial with a glassed-in front porch right next to it, with a modern kitchen and modern bathroom, and he never let them move into it because he

Ten Commandments against Abuse: Love without War

refused to connect the electricity and water. He just wanted his wife to look at that beautiful house every day, my father said as we pulled into their driveway, and touch that bit of modern heaven so close and so far away. He built that house just for her and he was beating her again, almost to death. She was a very old woman who had lived this way with him all of their very long marriage. They are dead now but I saw both the older house and the newer house next to it just a few months ago. I could not tell if anyone had ever moved into either. I don't know if anyone else knows that this is a monument to cruelty and interpersonal warfare.

Since then, I became more and more aware that the pleasantness of public spaces like schools, malls, parks, workplaces and churches are sanctuaries from the more private wars that take place in small homes and in mansions in this country and around the world.

If you wish to be aware, you can see people walking along transparent minefields or tethered by jewelry and tattoos, or flinching within magnetic, emotional, palpable yet invisible fences of prescribed behavior and habits.

If you wish to listen, you can hear scathing

and virulent salvos against the ego. If you don't turn away too quickly, you can see the bruises, the shell-shocked gait, and the calloused patches of faces where fists have landed habitually.

If you really wish to pay attention, you can see and hear the joy switch off when it is closer and closer to the time to leave the public place.

What you may not be able to avoid is the loud silence that follows learning that someone you know has died all too soon, fallen in their own domestic war. It is a loud silence full of the energy of the incomplete life, the one not yet lived, the one shelved. Five times, I have heard that grating silence that followed the death of women that I knew, richer and poorer women. It is the opposite of the calming silence I heard at the funeral for that very old man whose tormenting days were over. I never understood how he, a deacon in a large and historic church, could stand in the front of the congregation every Sunday to welcome people to God, knowing that the people he faced knew he was a wife beater. I never understood why the leaders of the church let him stand there in the first place, knowing that the right hand of fellowship that he extended was the same one that punched his wife that very morning.

In the nearly fifty years since that dark night in the driveway of those two houses, I have traveled to more than thirty-five of the United States and to nearly twenty countries. I cannot count the number of countries whose citizens I have had conversations with along the way. Many of them are atheists, agnostics, believers, priests, nuns, monks, preachers, deacons, teachers of many world religions, all of whom were people just trying to find their way through this life. I have heard more and more stories of abuse and too many of those stories are connected to pseudo-justifications based upon religions that claim a Creator God that loves humans.

In those fifty years, I have had conversations with people in North America, Africa, the Middle East, Europe and Southeast Asia and with people from South America, South and Central Asia, and Australia and Pacifica. In talking with people who follow many different paths to the Creator God or who don't believe in a god at all, I have learned that most of us share the basic idea of a beautiful life that can be attained by living fully into just a few rules.

Ten Commandments against Abuse: Love without War

In this book, we will take a journey through ten such rules to recover their lessons of love by sorting out pseudo-justifications of abuse that have been shared with me in those conversations. Yes, some people use religion to justify domestic violence but I suspect you knew that when you picked up this book.

Rather than name any one female or male victim of domestic violence, I am going to create a character to represent them all. Her name is Lizzy Strata. The name comes from an ancient Greek play entitled *Lysistrata* written in the fifth century BCE by Aristophanes. In this comedy, Lysistrata was a woman who thought that she could stop a war between Athens and Sparta by organizing the women. So, in this book Lizzy Strata will stand for a woman caught in an interpersonal war called domestic violence. You have the power to decide if this will be a tragedy or a comedy. We will take Lizzy through the ten acts, *The Ten Commandments against Abuse.*

Lizzy Strata could be anyone you know who is being abused, even you. The Lizzy Stratas of the world love God and God loves all of the Lizzy Stratas. But the Lizzy Stratas do not

Ten Commandments against Abuse: Love without War

know how to be loved God's way. Lizzy Strata-type people live in a spiritual state of the Nile where floods and droughts happen but things eventually reach a normal that is peaceful, healthful and full of life. Lizzy's normal state is the drought with its absence of peaceful, healthy and life-enhancing love. Lizzy Strata, and people like her, live in a state of denial.

You will encounter people who used to live Lizzy's life and sometimes they slip back to that spiritual drought or state of denial out of habit. It takes conscious work to stay out of that spiritual valley of denial. Sometimes it requires daily attention. Life is beautiful for Lizzy when she is not in that spiritual drought.

What is it like for Lizzy to live in a spiritual valley of denial about her reality or in a state of denying to others how awful her reality is? Lizzy lives in a state of slavery, one that the Creator God never intended. Many of the Lizzy Stratas that I have met believe that the Creator God knows about their situation but somewhere along the way they were taught that God-fearing persons show their piety by suffering through the abuse and their abusers may have been taught directly or indirectly that God ordained them to abuse. These ideas have been around for centuries, even millennia.

There are paths out of these abuse-supporting thoughts and one of those paths is through the Ten Commandments. Since these Ten Commandments are part of the story of the Hebrew people leaving slavery and abuse in Ancient Egypt, then that is a good metaphor with which to start Lizzy's journey out of being abused.

Here is the story that we will use to describe life in an abusive relationship. Once upon a time, Ancient Egypt was one of the most dazzling, sophisticated, cosmopolitan places on the planet. You could depend on a good harvest because the Nile River would fertilize the farmland every year on schedule. Life was fairly easy. And the fashions were excellent! You could purchase a beautiful home decorated in the latest wall textures with courtyards containing flowering trees and verandas and porches on which to gossip with your neighbors while the children played nearby. There was beautiful music in the air.

Ancient Egypt was a great place to be female. In the marketplace, you could purchase

Ten Commandments against Abuse: Love without War

dresses made of pleated chiffon and handcrafted jewelry made of gemstones from around the known world. Hairstyles, cosmetics and carved furniture were dazzling. We now know that in Ancient Egypt women had businesses and wealth of their own. Some worked from home and others worked nearer the marketplaces. There were daycare providers who would work in your home while you took care of business. As a woman, you could have it all. Life in the state with the Nile River was absolutely marvelous.

So how does slavery enter this story? According the version recorded in the Bible, Abraham's descendants moved to Egypt to escape a time of famine and distress. Ancient Egypt was a haven, a golden opportunity and a chance to live large. As generations passed, however, the Pharaoh of Egypt felt threatened. It does not matter if the threat was real. He *felt* threatened and he was determined to keep the upper hand. The Ancient Egyptians began taking advantage of the Hebrews. They knew they were a dependent people who had little negotiating power and no one to champion them. They were isolated. They had no local support.

Ten Commandments against Abuse: Love without War

They had no treaties or friendship alliances with any nation but the Ancient Egyptians. Isolated, the Hebrews had no ability to defend their rights as the Ancient Egyptians gradually and deliberately deprived the Hebrews of freedom, wealth and personal rights. They became enslaved.

So why didn't they leave while they were yet free? We don't know. Maybe their memories of the famine and hard times in Canaan were kept alive. Maybe those memories were exaggerated each time the story was retold. Maybe the children of Abraham convinced themselves that they just could not survive on their own back in the wilderness. They imagined discomfort and hunger. They did not remember that Canaan was once a great place to live. They held on to the fear and forgot the positive memories and possibilities.

The Ancient Egyptians might have filtered or distorted diplomatic reports from Canaan. They might have planted rumors that it was a terrible place. Exaggerating fear would have been a great way to cripple the Hebrews' sense of independence and to overcome their personal will. By doing so, the Ancient Egyptians could

Ten Commandments against Abuse: Love without War

position themselves as great protectors who only required unquestioned loyalty and obedience.

Thoroughly frightened out of striking out on their own, the Hebrews may have accepted slavery in exchange for freedom from worry. Besides, working as slaves in luxurious Egypt was not so bad, was it? The weather was nice. The food was good. They were not whipped every single day. So they gave in to the Ancient Egyptians' earliest demands. Then the demands became worse. More work. Fewer benefits. No rest. No respect. Why should the Egyptians respect a people who were afraid to live an independent life? Why not take advantage of these people? At first glance, it looks like the Hebrews and the Egyptians are both exploiting the other. It looks fair, doesn't it?

Remember, though, the Hebrews put themselves in a weak position by not walking away at the first red flag of warning and the Ancient Egyptians were keen on taking advantage of the Hebrews' weakened self-esteem and fear-filled mindset. Imagine that the Hebrew labor union chose a spokesperson to ask for better conditions.

I can hear a Pharaoh respond like the spouses of the many Lizzy Stratas that I have met, saying "You don't like working here? Then leave. But you know you will never have it as good on your own as you do with me. Don't I feed you? Don't I clothe you? Don't I take care of everything so you don't have to worry? I've done this so long that you don't even know how to make it anymore without me. Go on and leave. The door is open. But you won't make it and you'll come crawling back to me. And if you do, I promise I won't be so nice to you."

You know what happened in the Bible story. The Hebrews stayed. They forgot that they were once an independent people who could do business on their own. They forgot that they came to Ancient Egypt by choice. They forgot that there were alternatives. They only heard those hurtful words thundering in their head so loudly and so obsessively that no other message could be heard. The Ancient Egyptians played a head-game so well that they didn't have to use chains to keep the people. The Hebrews in this version of the story gave their consent to be enslaved by staying.

Confident in the power and control that the Hebrews *gave* over themselves, the Ancient

Ten Commandments against Abuse: Love without War

Egyptians pressed further. Now they threatened their children. They killed their parents with neglect. They beat them, whipped them, and starved them. And finally they did kill their children right before the Hebrews' eyes.

Why in the world did the Hebrews stay so long?

They looked around and saw luxury. They looked down when the whips came. They never looked the Ancient Egyptians in the eye as equals because they had surrendered independence for comfort however the Hebrews defined it.

The Hebrews daily sacrificed themselves on an altar to Pharaoh in their mind.

The Hebrews treated the Ancient Egyptians like gods. Yes, Pharaoh told everyone that he was a god. But saying so meant nothing until someone believed him. The Hebrews forgot that God was God. Or maybe they thought God was too far away or that God does not exist. Maybe they feared the human-god who whipped them. Maybe they wanted to be courageous enough to fight for the dignity and respect offered by God who loved them but they just did not believe that they had a chance.

Then there was the very real fact that their very lives were now in danger from Ancient Egyptians who refused to let them go.

The Ancient Egyptians in this Bible story had a good thing going on: the Hebrews did their dirty work and controlling them gave people like Pharaoh a psychological ego boost. There was no reason for the Ancient Egyptians to go back to doing that work themselves. The Ancient Egyptians were now dependent on the Hebrews for their daily needs. Ancient Egyptian luxury depended on Hebrew labor. So, Ancient Egyptians had to remain god-like to control the Hebrews.

To stay in the comfort zone near the Nile, the Hebrews denied the love of God.

This is what it means for the Lizzy Stratas to be in a state of denial and of slavery. Lizzy may have chosen to worship her abusers as if they were gods. Lizzy may not have even been taught another way of living.

A hard lesson to learn is that some Lizzy Stratas in this world, rich or poor, volunteer to be someone's slave because they think the trade-off for comfort and security is a bargain. Another of the many realities is that some Lizzy

Stratas were coerced into their situations by family members or those who claim to be looking out for Lizzy's best interest. Still another is that Lizzy lives in a community where it common or traditional for women to be dominated by ***men who were raised to think they are god-like Pharaohs in their relationships so they must rule over women like benevolent or cruel slave-masters***. Men and women in these cultures or frames of mind are both out of order with the first commandment.

3 Steps toward God's Promised Land

So how do the Hebrews and Lizzy Stratas get out of the Ancient Egypt that is their unhealthy relationship?

1. Exchange their god-like Pharaoh for God.

The first commandment has the answer. It is very simple and it is incredibly hard: Lizzy has to change gods. She has to look her Pharaoh in the eye. She has to take off Pharaoh's mask and see that beneath all the pomp and boasting and gestures and threats, there is no one but a human who is constantly worried and insecure, fearing the day that Lizzy stops working for them. In the long run, **Pharaoh is more dependent on the slave than the slave is dependent on the Pharaoh.** Lizzy's spiritual-Pharaoh knows that. So, in order to keep Lizzy from looking up and seeing the real Creator God, Pharaoh must beat Lizzy down and use words and threats and physical harm to keep hold of her. And a jealous Pharaoh may even decide that if Lizzy won't work for him/her, s/he'll make sure that Lizzy won't work for anyone else. They will kill their Lizzy Strata. **Pharaohs do not respect slaves. Remember that. Pharaohs use slaves and discard them for another. There is always another slave on the market.** The many Pharaohs of the world know this and therefore they have no incentive to change themselves. They just wait for the next slave who will see the Pharaoh as a god.

So here is Lizzy's dilemma. Who is Lizzy's god? Is Lizzy trying to negotiate the terms on which she will continue to be Pharaoh's slave? Is she still sacrificing even a fragment of herself on an altar to her Pharaoh in hope that the sacrifice will appease him/her? How long do you think that will last before Lizzy must make an-

Ten Commandments against Abuse: Love without War

other sacrifice, ultimately even her very life?

When the Lizzy Stratas of this world, male or female, are beaten down by their Pharaoh, they can't look up any more than that very old woman did on that very dark night in her driveway fifty years ago. And Lizzy can't look around to see that there really are other places with rivers and food and work and homes. There are even luxuries out there. So what if she doesn't have all the things she had with her Pharaoh in her virtual Ancient Egypt? Lizzy has her life. Lizzy will have her peace. And Lizzy has the Creator God's respect and love.

2. See yourself the way God sees you.

The second lesson for Lizzy Stratas as they leave their Ancient Egypt is to learn to see themselves the way God sees them and not the way their Pharaoh wants them to see themselves. Pharaoh will not be happy when s/he senses that their Lizzy is beginning to look up. S/he will use all kinds of tricks to stop Lizzy from leaving. Some hide the car keys, empty Lizzy's bank account, get her fired from her job, spread rumors that Lizzy is crazy, bruise her face and body to create shame of going out in public, and/or make Lizzy feel bad by flaunting an affair. Even after our Lizzy Strata is successful at obtaining a divorce and moving on with her life, Pharaoh might still throw words, threats and fists at her. Pharaoh may take the children away, teach them to despise Lizzy, or even kill the children. There are many ways in which a Pharaoh will attempt to cripple Lizzy. Pharaohs are desperate. They will do anything to keep Lizzy from seeing herself as the strong, beautiful human God made.

When Lizzy Strata sees that God made her as a special and unique person with a valuable destiny to perform in this world, she will learn that she has power from Creator God to live out her full life. Lizzy Strata will learn that she is the equal of her Pharaoh and not inferior. She will stand tall and look Pharaoh in the eye.

In the harsh reality outside of public spaces, **it can be dangerous for any Lizzy to look any Pharaoh directly in the eye. Be careful about advising any Lizzy Strata to literally look her abuser in the eye. If she lives through it, she may have a black eye or worse for doing so.** Judge Lizzy's circumstances carefully. Sometimes you and Lizzy must be secretive about her new sense of self-strength.

Remember, Lizzy's Pharaoh knows that s/he is human, and insecure, and afraid of losing the good things that Lizzy bring to life. When Lizzy really understands that her Pharaoh is a frightened, dependent adult, then her Pharaoh will move in her mind from being a god to being only human. That transition in thought can be the opening of Lizzy Strata's gateway to liberation.

3. Have no other gods but God.

The Lizzy Stratas of this world, female and male, struggle several times a day and may be constantly aware of their daily choices to serve their Pharaoh or to serve God. The first commandment says that she must have no other gods before God.

If you are helping someone like Lizzy, you must also be realistic. Because Lizzy lives with a Pharaoh, she needs to plan to leave her spiritual Ancient Egypt. You have to know how hard-hearted Lizzy's Pharaoh is. You have to know the risks she faces, that her children and dependents face and the possible risk that you may face for helping her. In this struggle to dethrone the Pharaoh in her life, she wins by leaving Ancient Egypt alive. Be careful. Remember, there are Pharaohs who will kill before they see Lizzy leave.

If your Lizzy Strata is in a potentially lethal situation, help her to be liberated in her mind and heart until she can liberate her body. ***Get professional help involved. Call the Domestic Violence Hotline or your local domestic violence shelter.*** If your Lizzy is not in a potentially lethal situation, be grateful and be cautious in case her situation is deteriorating. Pharaohs rarely stop pretending to be a god. Call the Domestic Violence Hotline to get professional help in assessing your Lizzy's situation.

Each day Lizzy Stratas must choose the altar where she will worship. Each day is an opportunity for her Pharaoh to make her sacrifice herself on an altar to him. For a time, Lizzy may have to perform some rituals that her Pharaoh's demands until her Red Sea opens so that she can leave her Ancient Egypt.

In her heart, she must disengage from her Pharaoh. This can take years for some Lizzy Stratas and it can try the patience of Lizzy's support network. On the outside, Lizzy must survive another day to reach the life God has for her or him.

God is fully aware of the entanglements of Lizzy's life and God has a plan to liberate her from her Pharaoh. She will face a daily battle to choose God and not go right back to being obsessed with her Pharaoh. She may find herself struggling against old habits and self-enslaving thoughts as she learns to keep her eyes on God and the life God has waiting for her. She will be tempted to sacrifice God's gift of new life. She may face some wilderness years when she misses the old comforts or luxuries of Pharaoh's home. Remember, she may be trading luxurious slavery for precious personal liberty and security however she may define it. Some Lizzy Stratas may find that they can keep more of their hard-earned money that their Pharaoh's won't spend. She may find that she will live more comfortably and safely without him. God has a network of people who will provide her needs and an amazing amount of her wants.

Once Lizzy Strata learns to follow the first commandment, she will become a survivor of abuse. Her soul will be free and may be free long before her body is. That will be a matter of time. Lizzy will have a daily struggle to keep her eyes on God. She has a choice. She can choose to follow this first commandment, to stop volunteering for slavery, to take herself off of her Pharaoh's altar, and to leave that comfort-trap in the Ancient Egypt that was her life. Lizzy Stratas of this world and you must be smart about liberating her body from her Pharaoh.

God's 10 Steps out of Martyr-Marriages.

Now if God used a ten-step plan to get the Hebrews away from Pharaoh, what makes you think that Lizzy can do it faster than God? Running on a whim can be dangerous. It can kill her. Taking the children away in an illegal manner might bring her up on charges of kidnapping. Please don't wait until Lizzy has to use one of these options.

If you are a pastor, preacher, minister, teacher, youth counselor or a community leader, you can purposefully examine your word choices, your social values, and your descriptions of relationships and roles in terms of the first commandment. If you have Lizzy Stratas in your office for counseling, it

may be because of your teaching. You need to examine yourself to see if you are supporting Pharaohs, directly or passively, purposefully or blindly, in order to determine what you have contributed to Lizzy Strata's predicament. Once you have examined yourself then engage with your colleagues in your field. Start conversations often with individuals and with groups. What are we as a community of thought leaders doing to reinforce domestic violence through acts of commission or omission?

Lizzy Strata has to admit that she is in an Ancient Egypt and that she is her Pharoah's slave rather than co-equal partner. This will take some education. She has to question, and then admit, why and how she allowed this to happen. How did Lizzy Strata give her partner permission to abuse her? It started when she said, "That wasn't so bad and look how I'm being treated now as an apology." She taught her Pharaoh that she was willing to trade herself and her body for luxury and comfort and security, however that appears in her life.

The longer Lizzy Strata stayed, the more her Pharaoh came to depend on her/him. That means s/he became more insecure and more determined to keep Lizzy. Lizzy has to stop denying her predicament early. And as long as Lizzy is breathing, it is not too late. So what does she do? How does she leave her Ancient Egypt?

The Hebrews had help getting out of Ancient Egypt and so does Lizzy: God if she believes in addition to professionals who are trained to help. Lizzy has to learn to be her own advocate and her own Moses. She has to speak up to the right people. She must take off her own mask and tell someone that she and her children and dependents are in trouble. Not everyone will listen to Lizzy, especially if she is leaving early when the abuse is verbal, financial and emotional. By the time Lizzy approaches you for help, there is no way to know how many people ignored her pleas over the years. For Lizzy, there are teams of trained people who know the law, who can speak for Lizzy, and who care to help her. You, if you care for the Lizzy Strata in your life, may have to call the **National Domestic Violence Hotline at 1-800-799-SAFE**.

First, Lizzy must put all the clues together to determine if she is in a martyr-marriage. Some people call these "red flags." She may have all of the latest fashionable goods, clothes, furniture and vacations. She may think that a man deserves to be a little angry now and then from the stress of providing these things for his family. Then again, Lizzy may be the only one who thinks that these clues add up to an abusive situation. Verbal and emotional abusers leave little physical evidence. You may even see the problem before Lizzy does.

Lizzy might be surprised that others see the problems that she is having. Appreciate the amount of courage it takes for Lizzy to admit to herself and to you that people might ever so gently be telling her that her marriage is not right. She might be missing the clues and hints out of pride and denial. Is her Pharaoh behaving wrongly and not respecting her? Is she trading pieces of her self-esteem and ambitions to appease him/her? Is she humiliated or isolated or afraid? These are not normal emotions to have in a day. They are warning signs that God put in each of us. A good partner will build your self-esteem, respect your dreams and work to make her happy. If you see that Lizzy's partner leaves her sad, crying, or feeling no emotions at all, she might be sacrificing herself on an altar to a Pharaoh.

Once Lizzy finally stops denying that she is in a martyr-marriage, you may discover that you and she have a lot to learn. Read what you can find about abused partners and signs of abuse. Study some of those advice columns in the paper seriously to learn more clues. Be aware of other women's experiences. Discreetly share what you've learned with Lizzy

I knew a woman who was ultimately killed by her Pharaoh. She found the courage to leave for a safe house and took her daughter with her. Then, she wrestled with teachings at her church that encouraged her to elevate her Pharaoh to god-like status. She moved back to her marital home to appease her Pharaoh, to turn the other cheek, and to pray him to salvation while he beat her because that is what her church falsely taught about male/female relationships. On the other hand, she was counseled at the safe house that her Pharaoh had broken his marriage vows and that this freed her from staying in the marriage. Unfortunately, she was counseled in her church that she could force her Pharaoh into salvation and kindness through meek submission to his beatings. She put Pharaoh above herself and above her role as a mother to a young teen-aged daughter. If she had valued them all as equal, she would not have gone home. She would have started a new life. She could only see as far as pleasing her Pharaoh. She became a martyr on his altar. She did not understand fully the first commandment. Pharaohs have free will, too. Her Pharaoh shot her in the head right in front of their daughter and his mistress. Her daughter lost her mother to a false god.

Do you know a Lizzy Strata who is on the same track? If she stays in her martyr-marriage long enough, her Pharaoh might kill her, only to find another partner just like her who will replace her.

So what is the point of dying for Pharaoh? Think of the children and dependents. Ask your Lizzy if she wants to take the risk that her Pharaoh will find a nice person with good values to finish raising your children after Lizzy is dead? Be prepared if her self-esteem is so shattered she thinks it might be a good idea. This is a dangerous and a sign that professional help is needed very soon.

Ten Commandments against Abuse: Love without War

Chose to live! Lizzy needs to hear this. Remind Lizzy that she/he can only do God's work if she/he is alive to do it. Giving Pharaoh the option of killing or isolating her puts Pharaoh's will ahead of God's will for Lizzy's life.

What will it be like to start life over after living in a Pharaoh's Ancient Egypt? It may be tough but life without a Pharaoh has the promise of getting better. Look at the Bible story again. The Hebrews had money with them when they left Egypt. If Lizzy recognizes her situation early enough, she can make plans and put them into action.

Here are some strategies used by some women who successfully left their Ancient Egypt. Every time that their Pharaoh hurt them, they would take some grocery money and buy savings bonds. There are some that are long term investments that can be cashed in a few months. It looks like a retirement plan instead of a get-away plan. Go to school and get new job skills to support the children. Buy a few items like additional pots, sheets, or put things in storage boxes to tidy up the house but also to make a quick get-away. Find a way to visit a legal clinic or a domestic violence shelter to learn about the laws regarding protective orders, custody, access to the children at school, medical records, etc. It is important that Lizzy is not accused of kidnapping the children. More than anything else, be ready for that opportunity to leave.

This advice can be very hard to follow for Lizzy's who have Pharaohs who are skilled in the craft of isolating their partners. Some Pharaohs insist on living in places where Lizzy will know no one but him. Whenever Lizzy develops a community of people who care about her enough to tell her that she is being abused, these Pharaohs will move household in a heartbeat or destroy Lizzy's social circle. Pharaohs are more jealous than God.

One of those formerly abused women shared her exit story with me. She noticed that her Pharaoh was graduating from verbal and financial abuse to physical abuse. She knew that it was time to stop praying and time to keep the first commandment. She used some of the money she saved to pay a lawyer to draft a separation agreement. The lawyer was sympathetic to her situation and charged her only for a consultation appointment. She set a standard for a condition that would let her feel safe enough to return to him. She insisted that her Pharaoh take anger management classes. That is when she learned how little she mattered to him. Her Pharaoh showed her that she was not worth the change in his behavior. He never attended a class. So, she filed for divorce and was awarded custody of the children.

Lizzy Stratas are in the most danger when they leave. It is crucial to get legal advice before leaving or at least sneak out to a counseling center to get advice. For Lizzy Stratas who are very isolated and can't leave home, call a hotline like the **National Domestic Violence Hotline at 1-800-799-SAFE.**

The point of the story is that this woman planned her escape. She saw what was coming down the road and that she was not safe. Like Moses and the Hebrews who packed their things and left Ancient Egypt, this particular Lizzy Strata also planned. If planning was good enough for God, it can be a good idea for Lizzy Strata if she has the luxury of time to do so.

But what about the children?

There is no standard answer for this. In some cases, the children are safe from Pharaoh's anger. In some cases, the children are also targets of that abuse. Then there are Pharaoh's who use custody as an opportunity. One Lizzy Strata was ordered by the court to let her Pharaoh pick up the children from her house. When she opened the door to let the children in, he barged into the house and beat her. This happened several times. No matter how long she took to open the door for the children, he would wait. Finally, this Lizzy went back to court and had the order changed so that exchanges happened at a public place but it was too late to prevent the emotional scars to the children. Most Pharaohs are ashamed of beating their women in public. I have seen three exceptions to this in the US and in England. Nothing is standard about Lizzy Stratas' situations and any situation can turn lethal.

Would it not be better if children were taught about co-equal relationships?

There is a story that I have heard from people who follow Judaism, Christianity and Islam. In the Biblical story of the creation of humans, Eve was created from Adam's rib. The storytellers all said the following. Eve was not created from Adam's foot so that he could not walk all over her. Eve was not created from Adam's skull so that she could not walk all over him. Eve was created from Adam's rib so that they would walk side-by-side through life, partners who cherished each other's hearts. In this story, Adam was neither god-like nor superior to Eve. The story is about first commandment.

Trouble happens when Lizzy Stratas elevate partners to be gods who must be obeyed ahead of the Creator God. The sooner Lizzy Strata sees that her partner's sense of self is the god-like status of a Pharaoh, the better it will be for her, the children and their dependents. Better may not mean more material things or more money. Better can mean a more peaceful, respectful, and love-filled life. Lizzy must stay alive because every day that she lives is a day of victory for Lizzy and God.

Chapter 2
The Second Commandment

You shall not make for yourself any idol, or any likeness of what is in heaven or above or on earth beneath or in the water under the earth. You shall not worship them or serve them; for I, the Lord your God, am a jealous God, visiting the iniquity of the fathers on the children, on the third and the fourth generations of those who hate Me, but showing loving kindness to thousands, to those who love Me and keep My commandments.

Lizzy Stratas and Pharaohs are excellent actors and keepers of secrets. Their lives look perfect to everyone. Sometimes in public, you might see Lizzy get a reminder from her partner about how good she has it whenever she questions the way she is being treated. When Lizzy tries to tell someone that things are not right, she is quickly told that she has it all with Pharaoh and what more could she want. This is what happens when living a material life and worshiping idols but there are other kinds of idols that affect the Lizzy Stratas and the Pharaohs in this world.

Over the last twenty years, I had few conversations about domestic violence and church practices with some male pastors of churches of different denominations ranging from Catholic to Baptist to non-denominational and non-Christian. All of them agreed that domestic violence was wrong.

Most of them agreed that men are a woman's Roman-styled demi-god when they said things like these statements. "Men are the head of the household. Women are to submit to men. Women and men are equal but women cannot be ordained ministers or deacon or trustees." One of them even said that women cannot teach men in Sunday School. A couple of them said that men are supposed to submit to their wives but they were rare.

The conversations continued. I asked them if they quoted more from the first four books of the New Testament or more from Paul's letters. Paul won the popularity contest. That question sparked conversations about seminary training, the lives of the disciples, the antiquity and assembly of the Bible from Aramaic, Greek and also comments upon the Latin Vulgate version. If I asked a question about something Jesus said, the answer was usually grounded in something that Paul wrote.

After a while, I asked them, "Which one is smarter, Jesus or Paul?" They paused. Well, Jesus of course," they each replied with confidence.

Then, I asked, "Why do you spend so much time teaching from Paul instead of from Jesus. Do you prefer Jesus as the silent lamb led to slaughter so that you don't have to follow his teachings?"

They wriggle, like little boys with their hands in the candy jar that they are hiding behind their back. "But Paul is so eloquent or deep or such a highly trained attorney" were the various responses.

"Oh," I said, "then Paul must be smarter than the Son of God."

On that statement, you can hear the tires screeching on the runaway bicycle of their pride in outdoing the legalisms of Paul the Roman citizen who used to persecute followers of Jesus' teachings! Then they start the rapid back-pedaling to Jesus over the motocross terrain between Jesus and Paul.

As the conversations ended, I dared several of the pastors to preach strictly from the teachings of Jesus for a year, for six months even, without referring to a single thing written by Paul the Roman citizen. None of them said they would give it a try. The closest I have ever gotten to a yes from such a pastor was a promise to spend a year of personal Bible study reading and re-reading the book of Matthew. The reluctance to let go of Paul and the preference to ground sermons in Paul's letters over Jesus' parables and sayings leads me to think that some people have made a god out of Paul and then they devote themselves to showing off that they can talk like Paul and reason like Paul until their congregations revere such pastors into god-like status.

Jesus is just a silent lamb to slaughter and that, to me, seems very un-Christian.

I have had similar but fewer conversations with people of other faith persuasions including Hinduism and variations of the Yoruba religion.

Ten Commandments against Abuse: Love without War

There are some experts in these religions who are so impressed with their mastery of doctrines and commentaries that they have lost track of a truth so universal that one might be able to trace it back through centuries and even millennia. One of the themes that emerged from these conversations is the loss of gender equality and the rise of male dominance.

All three of these scenarios (Lizzy's life, the Paul or Jesus survey, and doctrine above equality) share something: idolizing men into something superior to women.

Let me bring it back to how this idolizing is practiced in many Christian churches and compare this to the second commandment.

The second commandment can be the hardest commandment to learn.

Suppose Lizzy Strata was raised in a typical Catholic, Orthodox, Protestant, non-denominational Christian church. The girls and boys in Lizzy's church were raised in a tradition in which they were trained that women must be submissive to men. Men, they were taught, were more accountable to God and men could preach. Women could not preach. Women were not supposed to wear pants, especially inside of the church, for that was a sin of cross-gender dressing. Boys learned to enjoy the freedom of sitting with their knees wide apart or an ankle rested on a knee. Their trousers protected their modesty. Girls learned that their freedom was lost as they donned higher heels, girdles and shapewear, and skirts that made them vulnerable to involuntary immodesty on breezy days.

During church services, the children learned that women's lives were restricted and men were superior by watching the adults. When sitting on the dais behind the pulpit, men could sit with their knees widely separated. On the few occasions when women sat on the dais or platform, they had to cross their ankles, pinch their knees together, and place their Bible or purse on their lap to keep their skirt from rising up. Men could relax during the three-hour service. Women had to hold their bodies in a contorted position for three hours. This torture was the price women paid for daring to rise with men to the dais. Then, there was always the potential embarrassment of exposing one's undergarments which were at eye-level to the congregation. Deacons sat on the front row where they would get first peek at the hidden regions of the ladies on the dais. Deaconesses sat on the second row, not necessarily behind their husbands. Women took a back seat to men, any man. The only exception was in the choir loft where men sat on the highest tier and women were below them. Everywhere, one was reminded of the false belief that men were superior and more godly than women.

Jesus and even the prophet Mohammad got into trouble when they taught men that God demands they respect women and that women are equal to men.

Idolizing men into Pharaohs by giving them the privileges of god-like status really does curse a family. When we invest in materialism or fashion or the Hollywood life or male dominance to the point that we sacrifice some part of our lives, our relationships, and our responsibility to be kind to each other, then we have moved from enjoying life to worshiping false idols.

Lizzy and the boys and girls that she grew up with are under a lot of social pressure to follow the abusive power dynamics of the Hebrews and Pharaoh of Ancient Egypt. Boys have to learn to be mean instead of men. Boys are taught to stop loving the women in their lives as the price of manhood. Girls have to learn to accept the mean treatment. Neither boys nor girls would do this on their own. Boys and girls have scars on their souls from this bad education. They have to be taught this unnatural behavior. They have to be taught to make god-like idols of men who know that they do not qualify to be gods. God-like status constricts the boys as they grow into men just as tight shoes, girdles and skirts constrict the girls. In the pursuit of these unnatural roles, boys' frustration rises.

When these men pursue Pharaoh-like status, making themselves into idols, and when they find themselves falling short of the status marks, they lash out in their frustration at loved ones. Their inner struggle to be mean to the ones that they want to love boils over and scalds their Lizzy with heated words, addictions to numbing alcohol and drugs, constricted lives and physical attacks. Lizzy and her Pharaoh may hide this from the neighbors but it is harder to hide it from their children. Their children see their parents acting out the gender roles from church and they learn that being an adult means lash out at their own children and spouses. And so it can go on to the third and fourth generation.

In the second commandment, God calls people away from this cycle of frustration and interpersonal violence.

God is honest. God is jealous – God wants us all to himself because God wants us to stay focused on the path of social relations in the Ten Commandments. It is a path of least resistance and least stress. God wants us to enjoy the material things of this life. That's why God put the ingredients for those things on the planet. God also wants us to enjoy our time with each other. For people like Lizzy Strata and their Pharaohs, that kind of enjoyment might be a dream or something for the afterlife because they were taught to make their marriage a space of abuse.

Some Lizzy Stratas and Pharaohs have a very comfortable and luxurious home in which their drama takes place while others may have just a room with a roof where the abuse plays out. Some people from England, the Netherlands, Switzerland and Nigeria have taught me that they were raised to believe that violence within marriage is an ordinary thing. Those people also taught me that they never learned that people lived any other way.

These individuals accidentally taught me that they lived their lives imprisoned in an idea that violent relationships were the only ones on the planet. I have met other people from the very same countries who live in non-abusive relationships.

The difference between the two groups was this: Were men god-like or equal to the women in their lives?

When Lizzy Strata, at the beginning of this chapter, suggested to others that her marriage was not right, the responses from her Pharaoh and the others around her say more about the mental prisons that those people lived in rather than what their responses say about Lizzy's sense of right and wrong behavior.

When a community or family strays from the second commandment, they start to sacrifice the important people that God entrusted to them. Boys who are raised to be the Pharaohs of their Lizzy's life need to be re-educated into the gender equality of the second commandment. Boys know that they are not qualified to be gods and men know that they are not qualified to be gods.

How hard is it for a Pharaoh to abdicate and let God be God? Maybe it is not as hard as getting those Christian ministers I met to preach from the teachings of Jesus rather than Paul. Maybe it is not as hard as getting that minority of woman-bashing Muslim clerics to teach the equality of women and men. Maybe it is not as hard as getting the minority of woman-bashing Jewish, Hindu and Yoruba priests to teach the equality of men and women. These religious leaders are often doubly-trapped and god-like twice over: first in their vanity and second by the constrictions placed in their own minds when they were boys and girls.

The second commandment compels us to not turn little boys into Pharaohs. The first commandment compels Lizzy Strata to take herself off her Pharaoh's altar. It is not Lizzy's job to re-educate her Pharaoh. That is the job of community leaders and educators. Some Pharaohs who abuse would rather kill Lizzy and their children than admit that the parents and people who taught them were wrong. They would rather erase Lizzy from the planet than face their mistakes. Boys who are raised to become unqualified demi-gods have hurricane-strength torment in their souls and they have no idea of how to calm the storm because their vain preachers starve them of the loving message of Jesus and the Creator God.

Pharaoh and Lizzy want to get out of the hurricane of domestic violence. God wants them to get out of this false, human-created hurricane, too, and God wants them to live a human life.

If you are counseling a Lizzy Strata about domestic violence and leaving her Pharaoh, remember this: neither you nor she knows which how big that hurricane is that rages in her Pharaoh or if he will erase the anguish by killing her and the children.

When you are not helping a Lizzy Strata, ask yourself if you are producing another Pharaoh by what you, preacher or ordinary person, teach and by how you live.

Chapter 3
The Third Commandment

Thou shall not take the Lord's name in vain.

With Pharaoh dethroned in Lizzy Strata's life and perhaps even in his own life, that could leave in charge the God of the first and second commandments. Who is God and what can God do for you?

God is the Infinity beyond our understanding.

Some of us like the powerful God. We like to think of God as a secret weapon that we can unleash on those who displease us. "Watch out or I'll turn God on you like a super-soaking water cannon!" That sounds childish, but I have heard people pray like generals, ordering God to come and go, to attack and deprive.

Others order God around like a genie in a lamp – "Come out now, do what I say and then go hide behind the altar until I call for you again."

Some of us like a super-concentrated God – all the power but none of the infinity. We might deny God's infinity by limiting the time of creation to 144 hours some 6 thousand years ago. Does God have that kind of power? Absolutely. Do we have the right to rush God's work? No! On what grounds do we tell God that God cannot enjoy the slow unfolding of creation over billions of years?

Then there are those of us who like to keep God in a box – God can only see us inside of a Church. Once we leave, we tell ourselves that God is not looking at us anymore. Or we think that the only sacred places on earth are in the church sanctuaries while the rest of the planet belongs to us. We can litter the planet with gum wrappers and nuclear waste as long as we do not break the stained glass windows in the churches.

Some of us like a cheap God. We think God can turn our pennies in the offering plate into millions of dollars. Well, yes, God can do that. But God is not cheap and God is not stingy. God is precious and we are precious to God.

So why are so many of us ordering God to

damn people to hell so often? Or why are we saying God's name because we are too lazy to think of another word to express our emotions?

We know the story of the shepherd boy who cried "Wolf" just to see how long it would take for the villagers to come save him. He did that so many times that people stopped paying attention to him. In the end, when the real wolf appeared and a real crisis happened, no help came at all. He did not learn his lesson because he was too dead in the wolf's stomach to ponder the moral of the story.

Would it be awful if you called God's name so often, used God's name for an adverb or adjective so much that the name had no meaning coming from you, so much so that God decided not to answer your call?

That is not where the damage is going to happen, though. When we use God's name in vain, we are testifying to others around us that we use God's name like we use old towels to mop dirty floors. We mix the name with filthy language. All around us, unbelievers and weak believers look at our behavior and make decisions about God's importance, about the reality of God's existence, and about God's power based upon our behavior. We cheapen the value of God's name in the ears of the weak believer.

When we take the Lord's name in vain, we mislead non-believers. And when we do that, we curse ourselves. Their future choices are greatly impacted by the God we present to them when we take God's name in vain. We show others a super-soaker God, a weak God, God-in-a-box, a cheap God. "If that is all God is," the weak believer or non-believer may say after our cheap presentation, "then there is no hope for me and no advocate for me. I might as well find comfort where I can in a bottle or a needle. I might as well fight my own battles. I might as well die now." We never know when we are a person's last chance to hear from God before they give up altogether. When we take the Lord's name in vain, we fail our mission to others.

Taking God's name in vain ultimately puts a curse upon ourselves. Every time your Pharaoh or church tells you that you must be a marriage-martyr to show God's love, they are misleading you. God is too jealous to let you be sacrificed on a human-god's altar. God is too infinite to need this empty demonstration of obedience.

Ten Commandments against Abuse: Love without War

God is not happy with those who use God's name to convince believers to worship men. They are using God's name in vain. Each time they do it, they put a curse upon themselves.

If your partner abuses God's name, is your partner open to abusing you?

Ten Commandments against Abuse: Love without War

Chapter 4
The Fourth Commandment

Remember the Sabbath day and keep it holy.

I never really appreciated our Sabbath tradition until I went to a land without a full day Sabbath. I visited a Muslim nation and learned that the Holy Day of Friday lasted about three hours as one went to Friday prayers and then returned home for a big family meal. Afterwards, it was back to work. Saturday and Sunday were days off to accommodate the Western work week schedule. But they were not Holy Days.

Sabbaths are precious. They are gifts from God. God created us. God knows the strengths of our bodies. God knows what we often forget: our bodies have limitations. God designed a wonderful system in which our bodies replace worn or damaged cells without us thinking about it. Even this has a limit for we are destined to die. Each body has its own internal destruction system and our societies have added more methods of body destruction. It seems that we invent more destruction mechanisms all the time. Until the destruction program in our bodies completes its task, we have time to live. That time of living and enjoying life is so precious that God has commanded us to take time for living.

Sabbaths are God's gift. The commandment to honor the Sabbath and keep it holy comes from the moment of Creation itself, before humans were even created. Here is a commandment to be like God. When God finished the work of creating the universe, God paused to enjoy it. It is a simple formula: work, create and enjoy.

Lizzy Stratas and those who are looking to abdicate from god-like status might rediscover the Creator God by celebrating Creation Day. On a Sabbath day, be it Sundays, Saturdays, Fridays, Thursdays or any day when they can step off the work schedule and pause to do something to celebrate God's creation. Look for the beautiful and amazing things God made and left for us to enjoy. Walk in the woods or go to

Ten Commandments against Abuse: Love without War

the zoo. Celebrate the gift of being creative and do simple art projects so that when you are finished you can marvel at what you have made, just like God marveled at each phase of creation and pronounced it "Good."

When an artist says that the work is good, that means quite a lot. The labor in creating the art is over as are the anxieties and struggles to turn inspiration into something real. The "good" moment means the artist can rest. Creation Day is about creating and resting. It is also about sharing. Some artists share their works with others. Some are too shy to let others into their genesis moments, their places of creation. That is a shame, for even God shares the Creation with humans. If rest is good enough for God, then perhaps we are missing some joy by not sharing our creations.

Not all of us are artists in that sense. Some of us are mechanical. We work and make quality items. They may not be original. But the copies that we make are indeed made with care and quality. We make good things. We make good houses, good bread, good clothing, good cars, etc. We catch details in the paper and computer forms that we process in our office jobs. We deliver products on time. Our customer service is the best. Our students learn their lessons. Our patients are comfortable. We do good work.

It is what we do at the end of the work day that determines whether we are keepers of this commandment or if we think we are better than God.

Do we take a Sabbath? Do we stop to enjoy the end product of our work? For many people, this means the Sabbath day is a day to stay in church. Having the luxury of being in church all day is indeed a way to celebrate the work week. We worked so hard that we earned enough money to take a day off and be in the company of believers.

What about those of us who work seven days a week? How do we keep the Sabbath? We keep it by remembering to keep some kind of Sabbath in our week. We may only have three hours on a single day of the week. Do we use that time to reconnect with God and with our families? Do we use that time to mend our relationships? Do we take time to laugh and enjoy the world that God has created?

Sabbaths can happen in five minutes on a daily basis, if that is all that your schedule allows. Share a laugh with family and friends. Stop to watch a bird or admire some flowers or gaze at clouds and stars. Admire God's artistry in nature. Rest with God and celebrate the Genesis or Creation days. The point is: stop and enjoy. Five minute sabbaths do wonders for those of us who work two and three jobs. Let me explain.

Skipping a Sabbath habit can be bad for one's health. I learned long ago that when I work without taking even a five minute Sabbath, God will make me take a forced Sabbath: Ignoring God's advice messes with body parts: blood pressure, pinched nerves, and more. Remember, God created our bodies to repair worn out or damaged cells during rest periods. We have to stop moving and using energy to work so that our bodies can use that energy to repair our damaged bodies. If we do not rest, then the repair work does not happen.

We all know what happens when we let clothing, house and car repairs go undone: the problem gets bigger and the repair more costly, even to the point of the clothing, house or car being irreparable. At that moment, when we look at the estimate, we say, "I should have fixed that when I first noticed it."

Well, our bodies do the same thing. We must look at the damage that stress does to our bodies. When we are in fight-mode or anxiety-mode or never-resting-continually-rushing-mode, our bodies pump blood and nutrients to our motor muscles and away from our organs. Add to that the stress of domestic violence. We look fine on the outside, strong and fit. But inside, we are slowly collapsing until we have a break-down or a failed organ.

Often, we simple refuse to take a long enough Sabbath to go to the doctor and get a physical. If we cannot afford time for a doctor, we may rush past public clinics or health fairs where we can get free check-ups for diabetes, high blood pressure, glaucoma, etc. While we thought that working without ceasing was a means of providing for our families, we sometimes end up in the hospital, flat on our back, without a paycheck and our families are in worse shape than they would have been if we had stopped for that annual physical.

Missing a health Sabbath is dangerous for us and for our families.

The five-minute Sabbath is also good for our

mental health. When we work those jobs that take 50 hours or more a week, when we work two and three jobs, when we work seven days a week, we often feel like robots. Well, we go through the motions of life and we ignore our feelings and our relationships. "I have to pay bills and so I have to work," you might say. Does this mean that all workers are robots? We are robots when we fail to tend to our inner spirit or find quality time with our family and friends. That can lead to frustration or missed opportunities of feeling appreciated by the ones we work to support. We lose those links that make us human and our spirits more humane. It is not the work that makes us feel like robots. It is how we feel about ourselves and our relationships to those around us that define our robot-like status. Finding five minutes in a day of things that we must do to get by in this world is a big step away from self-abuse.

When we take a five-minute Sabbath, even if we are on the bus or caught in a traffic-jam, we remove our minds from the work mode. We let our bodies relax for a moment and send that much-needed energy and nutrients to our organs for body repair work. When we laugh with our family at home as we change clothes between shifts, when we take a minute to hug and listen to others, we have taken a vacation from work. We have stopped to celebrate God's Creation.

We are ordered by God in the fourth commandment to take a break and say, "This work is good because it lets me provide for my family and gives me five minutes to enjoy and share with them." That five-minute Sabbath, if it is all the Sabbath time we have in a week, is absolutely necessary to promote healing in our bodies and in our relationships on a daily basis. When the Sabbath is over, we choose to return to work.

Let me say that again. We *choose* to return to work. Choice is what keeps us from being robots. Choice is an act of self-love and a shield against self-abuse. That moment of choosing is the mental health break that can keep us from burn-out. Choice is what makes us human.

Ten Commandments against Abuse: Love without War

When God created humans in the Bible story, God gave us the choice to obey. Animals do not have that choice. Each time we choose to work and to labor until we reach the next Sabbath moment, we are a step closer to the ideal life recommended by God. The work must be done. That is absolutely true. If God worked, so must we if we are physically able to do so. You are right, the bills must be paid. As long as we see it as a choice to do so, we are not robots.

Choosing to work means that we have the choice to rest, be it for a day in a week or for just five minutes in a day.

Choosing to work means that we anticipate enjoying the product of our labor and that we have the pride of pronouncing our work as "Good." When we remember to have a Sabbath daily and a Sabbath day if we can afford it, we become more like God. Jesus put reminded us of this. "The Sabbath was made for man, and not man for the Sabbath." (Mark 2:27) This makes all the difference in the world because the fourth commandment teaches us to not abuse ourselves.

Ten Commandments against Abuse: Love without War

Chapter 5
The Fifth Commandment

Honor your father and your mother, that your days may be prolonged in the land which the Lord your God gives you.

Avoiding abuse is a deliberate act that affects our lives and the lives of those around us, people we know as the Lizzy Stratas and the Pharaohs in our worlds. Each day we make decisions on how to act. What will we do? What will we not do? What will we say? What are our hopes? Where will we go? Who is a friend? Who can we help? What is important? How do we stay on the abuse-free path God has designed into the Ten Commandments if we are abused by our parents or even our grandparents?

All of these questions run through our minds so quickly that sometimes it feels like we do

Ten Commandments against Abuse: Love without War

not go through this process of decision-making at all. Sometimes we act so quickly that we forget to listen to the answers to our questions. Some might say that we often act without thinking. That is not quite true. We do think before we act. Sometime we make a choice to ignore the thinking process. We then do things we regret. We apologize and claim, "I wasn't thinking." We might even claim that we are not responsible for what we have done or that our behavior is normal based upon the abusive behavior of the people around us.

For example, a person has a few beers, gets angry and explodes – hitting someone with words, fists, cars, or bullets. You might hear that person say one or more of the following:

- I was drunk.
- I wasn't myself.
- I wasn't thinking.
- I didn't mean it.

Too many times some of us hear these words from our loved ones. Too many times some of us say these words, even to the children in our lives. Once the words are out, they cannot be erased. The damage is done, like drops of water that cause metal to rust or stone to erode. After a while, the damage is visible. We cannot change the past.

Why do we do this? Sometime we choose to skip the thinking process and act in a familiar pattern. It might be the pattern that we learned in our childhood. Some of us were children who witnessed people using these excuses instead of changing their behavior. Rather than come up with our own solution or answer or new way of living, we get lazy and use someone else's answer.

In other words, we cheat. We cheat ourselves and we cheat our children. How? We deliver less than our best selves and in doing so we shortchange others. We do not make the best choice.

When we fail to think through our options, we miss an opportunity to deliver a blessing from Creator God to someone God cares about. We dam up the river of kindness and love that God designed. We miss a chance to enhance the lives of those around us by damming the recommended solution to the situation that will set in motion generations of goodness. We interrupt all of this by choosing to be lazy by just living into the same old abusive patterns of prior generations.

What can cause this? One answer is that we forget to honor our parents.

Oh sure, on Mother's Day and Father's Day we buy flowers, ties, cards and dinners. When our parents get old and ill, many of us make arrangements to take care of them. We pay for fancy coffins, flowers, and place photographs along with the funeral notice in the newspaper when they pass away. We put fresh flowers and flags on their graves on their birthdays and holidays whether we do it because of formal cultural traditions or out of our own informal traditions.

This is one way to honor mothers and fathers. We make them royalty for a moment.

There is another way to honor our parents. We can remember them.

What is the difference? We have to remember the life lessons we learned from our parents – good and bad. Most of us have happy memories of our parents. We learn from them a lot about the worthwhile things in life – the joy of family and community and living. These are great lessons to teach the children in our lives,

Ten Commandments against Abuse: Love without War

lessons they will draw upon as we in turn age and depend on them as we grow more helpless. (John 21:18)

Some of us have no memories of parents. For many reasons, our parents were not there. They may have died early through illness, warfare or accident. They may have gone to prison. They may have abandoned us. They may have given us to someone else. These are painful realities that some would rather forget.

Some of us have nightmares about the horrific things our parents did to us: the abuse, the neglect, and the verbal assassinations. (See the next chapter for more about this.) For some of us, our parents killed us a little piece at a time in many, many ways. The physical and emotional scars and hardships some of us have from our parents stay with us, cripple us or drive us for a lifetime to attain great or terrible goals.

How in the world does anyone keep the fifth commandment and honor such parents and grandparents, people who were not always honorable toward us and who created a state of warfare between us and them? Is it madness to do so? Sometimes our parents are our enemies. Sometimes, loving them blindly just brings us more pain and makes girls and boys into abused Lizzy Stratas. Loving these elders blindly means we might find ourselves on an altar to our parents, killing pieces of our bodies, our mental health and our self-esteem.

Jesus tells us to love our enemies. There are worthy sacrifices we must make to care for them. We give them whatever we have to share in keeping with Jesus' instructions in Mark 7:9-13. We have to find a balance between loving and caring for them and loving ourselves enough to maintain our goal of living the emotionally healthy life found in the Ten Commandments.

So far, for some of us, there seems to be little hope in remembering our parents. The fifth commandment promises that honoring even such parents will result in a longer time for us in a space God set aside for us. What kind of promise is this? Is this some kind of cruel joke?

Jesus said that this is the first commandment with promise. God said that by honoring our parents our days will be long in the land God gives us. Our lives are that Promised Land. Our parents are human. They made good decisions and bad ones. They climbed mountains and celebrated. They dodged predators out to hurt them and survived. Sometimes they were the predators. They set traps, fell into pits and stumbled over barriers. They had strengths and weaknesses. In the course of their lives, they gave us life.

Parents are an encyclopedia of life's events. When we remember them, we read their lives and respect the consequences of their actions. We honor the wisdom that they accumulated during their lifetime whether or not they practiced that wisdom in their life choices and in how they treated us and their own parents.

If we learn the lessons from their experiences, we acquire knowledge and wisdom. We can do so without having to repeat their mistakes. The information we gain from them becomes one factor in making our daily decisions about what we will do next. God promises us that if we include this information in our thinking process (meaning that we evaluate their behavior and use that to help us decide how to act), we will avoid one more potentially fatal trap in the road of life so that we can live another day. It means that we may live a better life in the days that remain for us. It means that our children will have even more wisdom to draw upon.

Sometimes, how we respond to the memories of our parents' lives can inspire us to become Pharaohs, too. Take a case where a parent cheated on a spouse or was an alcoholic. What if the female or male child responds by being an adult who is so controlling of the members of their own household that they become a Pharaoh who enslaves the family with other cruelties? What if the children respond to homelessness and poverty by being adults who hoards things, animals and garbage in the home, creating an unsafe living environment out of an intention to shield their own children? What if the children become adults driven to tyrannical perfection? It can take several generations to break the cycle of behavior in a family

The cycle can be broken in one generation through intentionally living the balanced life achieved by following all of the Ten Commandments.

This is a promise. A remembered pain or joy is the price to pay for avoiding another lived pain in our lives or someone else's life. Decreasing the pain and hardships in our lives is a blessing we can experience as frequently as we

Ten Commandments against Abuse: Love without War

remember to think before we act. This commandment frees boys and girls from becoming adult Lizzy Stratas or Pharaohs.

Ten Commandments against Abuse: Love without War

Chapter 6
The Sixth Commandment

You shall not murder.

Verbal assassins are everywhere. Pharaohs use verbal assassination as a first weapon against their intended Lizzy Strata. Verbal assassination damage has a long lasting impact on a person, much longer than a bruise lasts, and memory flashbacks make these attacks into repeater weapons. Some of us use words to partially kill and/or we are partially killed by words many times in a day.

Jesus tried to teach us about what we now call verbal abuse. "You have heard that the ancients were told, 'You shall not commit murder' and 'Whoever commits murder shall be liable to the court.'" That much is understood, except during times of war when we remove this restriction from our soldiers. Jesus took this commandment to another level. "Whoever shall say, 'You fool,' shall be guilty enough to go into the fiery hell." (Matthew 5: 21, 22b, NAS). Whereas acts of killing the body merited a trial before sentencing, according to Jesus calling someone a name is an immediate ticket to hell.

What is the sin of verbal assassination or name calling? There are many of them. When we call someone a name, we kill a piece of their self-esteem. We cause a piece of their spirit to diminish, to recoil, and to hide from further assaults and embarrassments. Name calling and verbal assassinations are designed to put people down and to diminish them.

Name calling and verbal assassinations are incredible weapons for they attack again and again every time the victim remembers the assault. This kind of attack can be as traumatic as physical abuse. The scar tissue that forms on the soul can be as disfiguring as knife wounds to the face. Scar tissue on the soul can cripple one as much as severed fingers or amputated legs. Scar tissue on the soul does so much damage that the injured person might use crutches such as drugs or alcohol or other addictive behavior. Some scarred soul pain is so great that the only way to numb it is to transfer that pain to someone else for a moment – that is, to abuse another person and let the passion of the abusive act cover the pain on the abuser's scarred soul.

There are so many ways to verbally assassinate someone. Dream killing is one. Now, there are some dreams that people have which should be stopped because they are destructive. Such dreams are forms of self-killing and they can involve killing others.

Other dreams are necessary to God's plan for peaceful human existence. We have to dream about kinds of employment and careers and moments of caring. Then, we have to make those dreams come true. We are back to the Creation story with God who had an idea and then spoke it into existence. Dreams are necessary before we can have art. They are also necessary before we can have invention. Dreams are necessary to *imagine* the act of farming, of forging, of manufacturing, of creating work for ourselves and for others. Dreams are necessary to imagine caring and nurturing and teaching. Dreams are the wellspring of ideas. Imagination has to be developed.

When good dreams and healthy ideas are

expressed, we as a society must cultivate those dreams because we will all benefit from them. Remember, we are discussing dreams that do not involve killing other people but that do have a multiplier effect of benefits to humanity like abolition and the United Nations Millennium Development Goals to end extreme poverty around the world. Good dreams and beneficial dreams are inspirations and gifts from God, even when the dreamer is an atheist.

If we kill the dreamer or scar the dreamer's soul to the point that the dreamer will not attempt to make the good dream a reality, humankind suffers and is diminished. That medical cure will not be developed. That source of clean energy will not be invented. That hybrid grain will not feed us. We all lose when we kill dreams. The impact of killed dreams on humanity is so great that Jesus tells us that verbal assassins are doomed.

So, are you a verbal assassin? Do these words sound familiar?

- "You ain't nothing but a . . ."
- "You won't ever be better than..."
- "What makes you think you are good enough to do that?"

Ten Commandments against Abuse: Love without War

What do the children in your life hear you say?

Does your son hear you and your friends talk about all men as evil? Then you are telling him to be evil and he will fulfill your wish because he does not want to let you down. You are killing his desire to be good.

Does your daughter hear you talk about all women as sex objects? Then she will become only a body to be used by men and women and she will never aspire to more in order to make you happy.

Dream killers affect those around them, their children, their children's playmates, their co-workers and their children's ability to love their own children. A verbal assassin chooses to maintain a hellish culture in the family. It is a cycle of living death and decreased joy suffered for generations until someone learns the lessons of this sixth commandment and breaks the cycle.

Well and good but what to do if you are the scarred soul? You can pray and express your pain to God, even if you can find no human to confide in. Then you have to make a brave decision. Many of us with scarred souls are unable to leave our dream-killers and verbal assas-

Ten Commandments against Abuse: Love without War

sins. We may be physically trapped in the home or the town without the means to leave just yet.

Right now, I am going to speak to you as a person. If you are continually assaulted, you may be in danger. Many attackers feel a rush from destroying you. In the passion of attacking, many assaulters feel like gods. You are the targeted piece of Creation that they want to control and destroy. Many attackers believe in a small god, a genie god, or a lightning-bolt-throwing god. They do not know that God is a loving God to the point that they join in God's love-plan. They are outside of God's peace. They choose to destroy and you are the target of the moment.

You may be in physical danger. If so, you must first acknowledge the danger of your situation. Next, you must get help. Choose your help carefully. Attackers have support networks, too. You must find help, even if you call the **National Domestic Violence Hotline at 1-800-799-SAFE(7233).** Would you be safer calling them before you tip off your attacker through the attacker's network of friends?

Now I am going to speak to you as a parent or care giver. Is anyone else sharing the home with you? They are victims every time you are attacked by your verbal assassin or Pharaoh. When a piece of your soul is scarred or killed, they are scarred, too.

So, what do you do while you plan your escape? You have to pray, pray like it is the first Passover in Egypt because the Death Angel has come to your door. Pray to recognize the fiery pillar in the form of the people sent to rescue you. Be ready to leave. You may have to leave without your identification. Try to leave some documents with someone in another home or state or in medical records or dental records at a public clinic.

While you are making your exit plan with your **National Domestic Violence Hotline** advisor or counselor, you have to recognize that you might be violating the second commandment. You might have made this partner into a Pharaoh-god and given your partner the power of life or death over your body. Maybe you have never been taught another way. Please read the Patricia Evans book to learn how you can avoid doing this the next time you consider entering a relationship.

The first time that you returned to your partner after the first assault you gave permission for the next assault. Attackers are methodical. They test the water to see how much you will tolerate from them. They believe that you consent to their bad behavior.

Verbal assassinations are often the first step used by an abuser. If you tolerate it, then they will proceed. If you let them limit your world, they will cage you with your consent. Don't consent. Don't make that partner a god.

If any minister tells you to tolerate abuse, change churches immediately. If you cannot, stop listening to that minister's advice, then read Matthew 18:15-18 for Jesus' teaching about being mistreated. The minister is preparing you for your own funeral and that minister is not teaching God's love. Some ministers give lessons in being gods. They often place limits on the power of God. They put God in a box and handcuff God by putting limits on God's infinity. They elevate themselves as the sole voice of God in your life.

Get away from these preacher-gods, at the very least in your mind if you cannot do so with your body. They are also verbal assassins who may be going straight to hellfire. You are not

Ten Commandments against Abuse: Love without War

obligated to join them.

If you are told that you must pray your abuser or assassin into righteousness through your humility while you are taking a beating, you must be careful that you do not give your abuser infinite opportunities like the very old lady with the very abusive husband in that very dark driveway. I was taught that marriage was eternal and that second marriages are adulterous. That comes from Matthew 19: 1-12.

I want you to read Matthew 19: 6 very carefully. "What therefore God has joined together, let no man separate." Did God put you in this marriage or did you ask God to consent to your choice of mate? If you are not safe, the chances are you chose your own partner and God accepted your decision. Do not blame God for your poor choice in marriage partner.

Next, turn to Matthew 18:15-18. There is a process for leaving a bad relationship. You have the right to complain and you have the right to be treated well. If you are being verbally assassinated, even before you even get to the point of physical assaults, you have the right to demand intervention. First, let your partner know that you want the behavior to stop. If it

Ten Commandments against Abuse: Love without War

happens again, take two or three people with you and have them talk with your partner. They may get through. If not, you may ask your church or the court or the police or doctors or social workers or the **National Domestic Violence Hotline** for help. *If at this point, the partner does not change, you have every Christian right to leave the marriage. Start the process early.*

Be careful about a partner who promises to change and then goes right back to the abuse. This is called the Cycle of Domestic Violence according to Lenore Walker. Do you feel like you are walking on eggshells or tip-toeing a behavior set by your Pharaoh? Does violence follow (physical, social, financial, sexual, or verbal)? Is there an apology when everything is all roses and champagne and presents followed by another time of walking on eggshells, another round of violence and another apology? Some Pharaohs do change. Some are just going through the romantic honeymoon motions of setting you up for another violent phase, a cycle that can lead to your death, your children's deaths, etc.

You have the right to unbind the marriage

Ten Commandments against Abuse: Love without War

because your partner has chosen to disregard marriage vows made to you. Jesus said in Matthew 18:18, "Truly, I say to you, whatever you shall bind on earth shall be bound in heaven; and whatever you loose on earth shall be loosed in heaven." You are under no obligation to treat your partner like a god and sacrifice yourself on that partner's altar. You may have to do so in order to survive until you can leave. You can leave and the sooner that you do so, the better. Marriage-martyrs are not Jesus' idea.

Anyone who counsels you to violate Jesus' exit plan may not be aware that they are asking you to violate the second commandment and risk your life. Remember, some preachers and counselors may also be victims of some Pharaoh's teachings. Instead, you must find a space of Sabbath where you can heal and recover and enjoy life. Jesus said that verbal assassins are doomed.

Fortunately, we all have an opportunity each day and all day to live by the Ten Commandments more fully. We have a daily chance to ask forgiveness and a daily chance to focus on God so much that living the commandments will come naturally.

Ten Commandments against Abuse: Love without War

Chapter 7
The Seventh Commandment

You shall not commit adultery.

There are some who say that adultery is only committed by a wife against a husband. Jesus does not say so. In Matthew 5:27-32, Jesus talks about bad reasons for divorce. For example, he seems to say that the only reason for a legal divorce occurs when a wife has been unfaithful. But a closer read of verse 32 shows that unfaithfulness is grounds for divorce. Jesus does not specify which partner had to be the offending spouse. In verse 27, Jesus clearly states that "everyone who looks on a woman to lust for her has committed adultery with her already in his heart." Husbands can commit adultery *by lusting* after any woman.

Intent is the moment the commandment violation is committed. In Mark 10: 11-12, Jesus says "Whoever divorces his wife and marries another woman commits adultery against her." It seems that the first wife was faithful and was abandoned by her husband. That is a crime against the first wife. Jesus said in Mark 10:12 that the crime occurs if the wife divorces her husband for another man. Notice that Jesus said that *a wife can* initiate a divorce. Divorce initiated for the direct purpose of acquiring a new sex partner is wrong.

Does this mean that the abandoned partner cannot remarry? Jesus talked with a woman at a well in Samaria in John 4:7-26. This is a woman who had been married five times. This was also a woman who was in a non-marital relationship with a man who was not hers. Jesus offered her living water. He saw that she was thirsty in her soul, looking for something in men that could only come from God. By looking for God in her new husbands, she may have imagined them to be more godly than human.

It must have been flattering for these men to be treated like gods, but after a while these men must have been under tremendous pressure to be god-like. Or, she may have chosen Pharaohs and left them. Or, she may have been a widow several times for any of a number of valid reasons. There is no telling what her situation was. There must have been more to her story.

One thing is sure: Jesus did not condemn her. I was taught as a child to see this woman as a bad, sinful person. I heard this version again within the last few months. She was an example that proved that you might as well stick with your first marriage, bad though it may be, because you won't find what you are looking for in another one. I was taught to be hopeless in my search for love.

Jesus offered to heal the spiritual thirst that drove her search.

What if the Samaritan woman refused to treat her husbands like gods? In verse 19, she is a sensitive woman of faith who has a gift of discernment. She perceived that Jesus was a holy man and thought him a prophet, a bearer of God's word and instruction. She was a woman of faith who worshiped God the way her ancestors did. She awaited the Messiah to end the discord between the Samaritans and Jews over the trivial matter of the location of worship when God is so much greater than that issue (verses 12, 19-20, 25). What if this woman refused to treat men like gods? What if she had the confidence and self-esteem to leave bad situations? She was still thirsting for a soulful relationship that had eluded her. Jesus did not call her an adulterer.

What about the woman to be stoned for adultery in John 8: 1-11? Here, the Pharisees brought a woman caught in the act of adultery and they wanted permission to stone her to death. Leviticus 20:10 requires that if a man commits adultery with a married woman, *both* are to be put to death. Jesus knew this law. He knew that stoning just the woman was an incomplete execution. He also knew that the men had turned the law into a tool of oppression for women. (In the denomination of my childhood church, unwed mothers were publicly shamed but I never saw anyone shame the men who fathered the children nor teen-aged boys who were not virgins.) So he asked for the sexual partner to be produced – all of the sexual partners who had ever been with her, apparently, for he said, "he who is without sin throw the first stone." None of them qualified. Perhaps all of them had committed adultery with her. I say that they were all guilty of adultery because that is the sin that was being examined and that is my only reason. Jesus took a stand against a culture that used and abused women as if they are disposable. Jesus took a stand against a system that did not hold men accountable.

Jesus chose not to condemn to her death but directed her to live a God-loving life. He did tell her to "sin no more." He taught her that she was worth far more than what her life had become. He knew the circumstances of her present and her past. He called her to respect herself as the creation God made her – a worthy woman.

He called for her to stop sacrificing her body on altars to men who thought they were gods.

Adultery is about abandoning one's spouse for sex with another person. Exodus 21:10-11 spells this out in the case of a man who brings another woman into his polygamous life. "If he takes to himself another woman, he may not reduce her food, her clothing or her conjugal rights. And if he will not do these three things for her, then she shall go out for nothing, without payment of money." Women are entitled to support and to sex. When a man compromises on his wife's sex life or the quality of her material life because of another sexual partner, when he kills that part of her soul, the wife is free to leave without paying him any compensation or expenses. This is Old Testament law.

Adultery happens when people pursue sexual exercise with someone other than their spouse. They abandon the bonds of intimacy that occur when God puts two people together. Adultery happens when we compare our spouses to other sexual partners because we leave the zone of intimacy in that moment. Adultery happens when we dilute the purity of the commitment that accompanies the sexual relationship in marriage.

Exodus 21 also tells us not to tolerate an adulterous spouse but to leave. Women can divorce when husbands cheat. These days, adultery can be a death sentence to the wronged spouse due to sexually transmitted diseases. It is possible to leave after the first instance. To stay longer these days is an act of raising a spouse to a god because one can surely die from adultery.

Adultery is an act of partial murder. It is not fair to the children who can lose both parents because of a poor interpretation of marriage as a life-long sentence and not a daily-earned privilege. When we all stop tolerating adultery, fewer spouses will believe that they can get away with it.

I know that what I am writing points to destabilized marriages. The marriages were already destabilized from within. I am writing this to you to let you know that Jesus never intended for you to live in a painful relationship. To live the Ten Commandments means to live a loving and respectful life in harmony with God.

No one should condemn or shun a spouse who follows Jesus' teaching to leave a marriage in which their soul was being killed a bit at a time by a spouse who had already left the marriage physically or emotionally.

Ten Commandments against Abuse: Love without War

Chapter 8
The Eighth Commandment

You shall not steal.

Pharaohs are good at suffocating their Lizzy Strata by depriving her and withholding what she needs to thrive so that she stays weak but alive enough to feed his ego. Sometimes this appears as financial abuse. Sometimes it is isolation through confinement, humiliation or belittling. On the outside, everything looks as perfect as a 1950s or a 1980s television show family. On the inside, there is as much depth to the family bliss as the set on which the television show was filmed. Why?

This kind of Pharaoh deprives the family of the oxygen of love, confusing the emotion with possession and stealing the very life out of the people living in that home. This kind of Pharaoh is someone who takes joy in starving the soul of Lizzy and the family.

Ten Commandments against Abuse: Love without War

Remember the rich young ruler who would not sell all that he had and give it to the poor? (Luke 18: 8-25) He kept all of the commandments. Where he expected accolades from Jesus, he was handed a spiritual mirror. Instead of seeing himself as a saint, the young ruler discovered that he himself was a Pharaoh in Jesus' mirror. Where did he sin? He sinned in his motivation for keeping the commandments. It must have felt good to boast of being so righteous. If he had been *willing* to sell all that he had, even some of it, and share with others, he would "have treasure in heaven." That was not the prize that he aimed for. He had the almost-perfect life but he missed a goal of the Ten Commandments – healthy relationships.

Pharaohs do not understand that they can get more out of their relationships by giving more of themselves. It is as if they are farmers who hoard seed but never plant in order to feed themselves or others. Some of them are unaware that they steal joy and love from themselves. They might be aware that they steal from their Lizzy Strata and the others in their life. In their mind, this is a rational choice because they see life as having only two kinds of

Ten Commandments against Abuse: Love without War

people: abusive users or the used and abused. Pharaohs command and abuse because they fear, or have memories of, being the abused one in the life equation they impose on Lizzy Strata.

Stealing from a loved one by omission and withholding is a sin several times over. Pharaoh and Lizzy break the first and second commandments by elevating Pharaoh to god-like status. Starving Lizzy's soul and self-esteem violates the sixth commandment. Starving Lizzy's soul and self-esteem also kills Pharaoh's soul in the process. Pharaohs celebrate their ability to steal from and to dominate their Lizzy Strata and in doing so they steal from God's plan of happiness for Lizzy and even for Pharaoh.

There is another theft that happens often: stealing joy. There are people who just cannot let anyone be happy. Where someone may be pleased to have a new second-hand car, the joy stealer will point out the dings, dents, and cigarette burns. Where someone is happy to own their first home of modest size or factory manufacture, the joy stealer leaves a magazine about designer mansions as a gift. These Pharaohs simply cannot *celebrate* with another person.

Ten Commandments against Abuse: Love without War

Joy stealers are a variety of joy-anemic, emotional vampires whose victims spread the sorrow. Such emotional vampires do not know how to enjoy life so they sap the joy out of others' souls. There are some people who steal joy by smothering it with woe. This is the kind of person who, upon seeing a co-worker in a new, flattering outfit, will point out the dandruff, cat-hair, or hanging thread. This is the parent who stifles a child's hard-earned C+ by comparing them to the class genius. There are so many ways to steal joy and so many things to steal. We steal when we withhold blessings and compliments. We steal when we fail to celebrate someone's joy. We steal when we isolate. Joy stealers are everywhere.

Sometimes, the slickest Pharaohs steal through financial, emotional, and verbal abuse, including hoarding loved ones by isolating them from society.

When Lizzy Stratas recognize abusive partners as joy-stealing vampires, they take a step toward seeing Pharaohs as humans and not demi-gods.

Chapter 9
The Ninth Commandment

You shall not bear false witness against your neighbor.

Insanity can begin with being a witness to something that never happened.

Joy-stealing, Pharaoh-god, abusive people who choose to abuse Christians depend on their victims being so nice that they would never speak ill of someone. They depend on their victims to forgive them an infinite number of times. Many Lizzy Stratas of this world were raised to never say a bad word about their partners and abusers.

As long as Lizzy Stratas are kept ignorant of the "escape clause" of Matthew 18:15-18, they will continue to give their Pharaoh an infinite number of chances to change until their forgiveness is made finite by death. They were taught to be doormat-christians. They were counseled to indulge their abusers' behavior. Lizzy Stratas can be found spoiling their abusers as a defensive strategy. It is a losing strategy that makes even God look weaker than their Pharaohs who use their Lizzy and slowly kill her self-esteem, shaming her in public, stealing from her, and gleefully destroying her.

Some of us, male or female, were raised in churches that teach us to martyr ourselves in the wrong way. It is one thing to die in the cause of spreading the Gospel. It is another thing to lay on the ego altar of an abusive human and be slowly sacrificed in a sadistic, emotionally and physically abusive relationship.

When Lizzy Stratas become marriage-martyrs on their Pharaoh's altar, they actually bear witness to a false religion that elevates the abuser to a false god. When Lizzy's support network of friends, family and clergy participate in this false religion by encouraging her to tolerate the abuse, they show non-believers that God's path is one of weakness and pain. We as a community of God-believers give a bad testimony about God when we side with Pharaoh and we might send people running anywhere but to church. By keeping silent about mistreatment, we deliver a false testimony about God.

People who enable Pharaoh's addiction to Lizzy's marriage-martyrdom by supporting the emotional vampire's fictions that rely on doormat-christians are also people who require that Lizzy Strata lives a lie. As people who claim to love and support Lizzy, such enablers may actually contribute to and facilitate depression and forms of insanity on behalf of Pharaoh. Lizzy Stratas use a lot of life-energy to maintain the false image of happiness, love and righteous living in order to survive, to please her Pharaoh and to please those who claim to be in her support network. Putting on a show of shallow happiness every day drains the life-energy from Lizzy's soul.

Lizzy might maintain this false witness for months or even decades, pretending to be perfectly happy on the outside when behind closed doors and within her heart she grows weaker. The light in her eyes grows dim. She may call it "growing-up" or "being tired" when in reality the darkness in her eyes is the accumulated lies that she piled up to cover her true self and her true feelings and her abuse situation. She really is suffocating spiritually and the dimming light in her eyes reflects her slow, spiritual death as she lies on the altar of her abuser's ego. She buries herself in the lies her abuser needs to maintain a public image of perfection. Bolder abusers are more honest in letting the abuse be seen and heard by others. Such Pharaohs have a false religion of their own: they themselves may live in the lie that everyone else is abusive.

Our abusers need to believe lies? Yes. They need them like a fish needs water. That is why abusers are so attached to their Lizzy Strata. They are like spiritual vampires. They need her life-energy to support the false impression that they want to project to the world. By being a false witness about her abusers, Lizzy is the primary mask or bandage to cover the abuser's real self. The more I've watched abusers, the more I am convinced that the abusers see themselves as defective, as lacking, as inferior, as puss-filled souls in the human family. They think they are so defective that no one can fix them. They see themselves as even beyond God's ability to fix them.

This is the lie that Satan has planted in some abusers' souls. It is very effective. This lie keeps abusers from turning to God. It makes abusers look only at themselves and they create a false image to mask their imperfections.

Abusers cannot maintain this mask on their own. They need someone to affirm the mask. They need someone to stand as a shield between them and the world so that no one sees the abuser's imperfections. Abusers need overly-nice Christians who were raised with marriage-martyrdom teachings to sacrifice their lives as a bandage covering the abuser's soul.

Abusers, because of Satan's lie to them, have a morbid fear and anxiety about being exposed.

This is another insanity, isn't it? Why would someone spend their entire life hiding from God who can fix them? That is not for us to answer today. Today we are trying to keep the Lizzy Stratas of the world alive.

Here is the marriage-martyr/doormat-christianity trap offered by some spiritual counselors who also ignore Jesus' escape clause of Matthew 18:15-18. What if Lizzy could stay with the abuser long enough to help her Pharaoh see the light of God? While this is based on a scripture verse, it has a sin-filled twist: It makes Lizzy into a god-like creature who can magically change her Pharaoh and it makes her responsible for failing to do so. That is the lie that Satan gives to keep Lizzy locked on the ego altar of her Pharaoh.

The abuser does not see the world that way. As long as Lizzy stays with the abuser, she remains nothing more than Pharaoh's bandage.

When she leaves, she exposes Pharaoh's flaws and that painful exposure leads some Pharaohs to kill Lizzy and even their children. As long as Lizzy and ill-advising counselors support the false image, they reinforce the twisted view of the world that the abusive Pharaoh has. This kind of doormat-christianity contradicts the teachings of Jesus Christ and violates several of the Ten Commandments. God keeps telling us to stop sacrificing ourselves to the abuser's ego.

Abusers know they are draining life-energy from Lizzy. Her Pharaoh knows that he is killing her a little or a lot at a time. The fact that Lizzy stays means she gives her Pharaoh permission to feed on her soul. The fact that she stays means that she thinks as little of herself as her family and community taught her. When she stays, when ill-educated Christian counselors advise her to stay, they confirm for the abuser that God does not really think any of us have any value because those who allow Pharaoh to be god-like emotional vampires must not believe that a real God exists. Such ill-educated counselors bear false witness about God to Lizzy, to Pharaoh, to their children and family, and to all of the people who attend Lizzy's funeral.

When we, in whatever capacity we have,

support the abusive Pharaoh's twisted sense of reality and their own low self-esteem, we bear false witness and lie about God. Jesus told us a story. He said, "look at the birds of the air" who do not farm nor do they keep barns full of food. God provides for them. "Are you not worth much more than they?" (Matthew 6: 26) Yes, we are! Jesus taught us that we are important to God, so much so that Jesus volunteered to die for us to show us this truth! So, now you have to make a choice: Do you choose God who knows that all Lizzy Stratas are important and valuable and worthy of good things?

Are you Lizzy? If so, are you going to stay with your abusive Pharaoh who cowers behind you only as a shield and distraction to keep Pharaoh from having to deal with his/her own imperfections and accountabilities?

Well, if you, as a Lizzy Strata, as an ill-educated counselor or as a support network person, are still clinging to a marriage-martyr, doormat-christianity like the very old woman in the very dark driveway five decades ago, I'll ask you one more question.

When the abusing Pharaoh decides that Lizzy has nothing more to give, what will happen?

Most abusing Pharaohs move on to the next

victim and they might do it over Lizzy's dead body. They won't blink an eye because their personal form of insanity turned their spiritual eyes off long ago as a survival tactic in the abusive twisted world they created for themselves.

Dear Lizzy Strata, you are only one more spiritual meal to you abusing Pharaoh. You are disposable. You are replaceable. You are only temporarily important. And then, you cease to exist.

Let me add more. You abusing Pharaoh never saw the real you. The abuser only saw the useful you. Your dreams and goals never mattered. Your feelings never existed. You have never been more than a meal, a source of warmth, money, shelter, shield and services. You only provided something the abuser needed. The abuser will walk away from you. Or, in some cases, the abuser will dispose of your dead body when the abuser is finished feeding off your life-energy. I'll be very clear here.

Some abusers actually kill their Lizzy Strata and her children.

Staying with an abuser is a form of suicide, whether spiritual or physical, and this violates a commandment against killing.

What can be more of a false witness to God than Lizzy's consent to be treated so poorly?

Now, **here is the dangerous part**. Lizzy Strata may be in physical danger. Lizzy's children may be in physical danger. In this case, you may have to support the lie on the outside while Lizzy pursues the truth in her/his soul as Lizzy switches from the abusing Pharaoh's false reality to God's true reality.

Dear Lizzy and Lizzy's friend, I hope you are reading this early enough to avoid this dangerous trap. If you did not get this message in time, as long as Lizzy is alive there is a chance to stop living the lie. Lizzy Stratas need help to get out of the insane world of abusing Pharaohs. You have to be wiser than you have ever been in your life. You have to find quiet places to listen for God's instructions. You have to bury yourself in the life-giving Scriptures. You may not be able to talk about this at church if your pastor preached marriage-martyrdom. More than anything, you need help and you need people on your side. **Call the National Domestic Violence Hotline.** Do it! Bear witness to the miracle of life that God gave you.

The way to God's life-plan for Lizzy Strata can be hard. Your Lizzy may enter new levels of poverty. Lizzy, you may have to leave everything you know, including family members who believe your abusing Pharaoh's false image. They may tell you that you are crazy to leave such a good person because they only see the mask that you helped create for your own your survival.

You may be surprised by the reaction of people in your community when Lizzy leaves Pharaoh. Some may refuse to believe Lizzy's truth because she supported the lie for so long and may have done so with your help. They may not want to support Lizzy because they, too, are living a false witness in their own home and fear a more violent Pharaoh who is frightened by what Lizzy's Pharaoh goes through without his/her Lizzy.

When one or more Pharaohs watch another emotional-vampire Pharaoh go through withdrawal as his Lizzy leaves and survives without him, the community of Pharaohs may become more violent as they become even more insecure about being exposed as imperfect by their own Lizzy Stratas who have cause for using Jesus' exit clause in Matthew 18:15-18.

Dear Lizzy Strata, you may be alone for a long time but as long as you are following God's plan out of abuse, as long as you seek support from safe places like the **National Domestic Violence Hotline** and counselors who really understand domestic violence, as long as know and remind yourself that you are important, you will never be lonely.

God wants you to live and to be a witness to God's power to deliver people from insane, false realities. God is always with you! That is the truth.

Ten Commandments against Abuse: Love without War

Chapter 10
The Tenth Commandment

You shall not covet your neighbor's house; you shall not covet your neighbor's wife or his male servant or his female servant or his ox or his donkey or anything that belongs to your neighbor.

If God ever puts blinders on us, those things that look like sunglasses on a horse, God does it with this commandment. Horse blinders are not designed to keep a horse from walking on its path. They are designed to keep a horse from being distracted. They are a short-cut for the person steering the horse and they take a lot of the tension out of a horse that just might be so curious that no amount of clicking or giddy-yapping or whistling will call that horse back to the road.

Poor horse! All that tension on the reins and so much strain on its neck just because it wants to choose its own path and smell a flower. That horse might not see the rattlesnake down the road or it might not understand that going down that hill with a fully loaded wagon is a recipe for disaster when gravity pulls the wagon and its cargo on top of the horse, leading to injury and maybe death for the horse and the rider. No, that horse is so focused on smelling the flower that it just is not looking for the safe road.

I have met a few wealthy Lizzy Stratas who were so focused on their own pretty flowers of material comfort, conspicuous consumption and status that they let their Pharaohs abuse them as long as there was a shopping trip or special event on the other side of the beating. I've met some work-a-day Lizzy Stratas who valued a marriage ring or status at church or a roof over their head or the appearance of familial love so much that they let spouses beat them like clockwork or molest their children or they let their own parents literally pimp them as prostitutes. These Lizzy Stratas explained to me some of the reasons why they willingly submitted to being abused. What these reasons have in common is coveting what the abusers have to offer. The difference between this group of Lizzy Stratas and the horse focused on the flower is that the horse would get away from the dangers next to the flower once it appeared.

We are like that horse sometimes. God wants us to take one path, the path marked by the Ten Commandments. We want to take the path that everyone else is on because we want what they have. Coveting kills our free will and makes us spiritual slaves to other people. When we covet what someone else has, we are not just choosing that item for ourselves. It becomes coveting when we surrender our choices to someone else. We are out of the self-control that the Ten Commandments teach. We surrender to another human, be it a Pharaoh, a commercial advertisement writer or some influencer in the in-crowd, and we elevate that human to a more god-like status.

If one reads the Bible, one finds that there are some very wealthy people and some very poor people in it. One also finds advice on how to handle education, finances and investments, and philanthropy. The problem occurs when the pursuit of things or status pulls us out of a balanced life. We imagine that we are in a competition with someone. That can be a healthy motivator.

God is very specific about this. Do you think your neighbor's house is the best? Don't try to buy it from them. Build your own. Are you attracted to your friend's spouse? Do not have an affair. What about your neighbor's cat? Or their stereo system? Don't steal it. It goes on and on. How many commandments do you have to break to get it or them? It becomes coveting when we want the one our "competitor" has rather than get another one.

So why is coveting a separate sin? When we lust for someone's spouse, we degrade our own spouse and that kills their ego, hurts our own marriage bond and that of the target of our lust if the pursuit is successful. When we brag that we wish our child was like the neighbor's kids, we might make our own feel less loved. When we work that extra job, not to pay the bills or to get something that we need but just to get that thing just like Joe and Angela down the street, we take time away from our own family who was happy without that thing. A missed day of family time can never be recovered. Every moment spent coveting is a moment that we do not celebrate living.

Coveting is wasteful, destructive, addictive and deceptive. It enslaves us. It creates unqualified gods all around us. Coveting hurts and we may not be able to repair the damage. It leads to family and money problems that could have been avoided if we were content with that which we have. Then we could work for something because we truly like it. We choose it. We know that getting it will not overburden our family nor lead to financial ruin. It will not destroy the balance and harmony of our relationships and family life.

A worse sin about coveting is that it is a gateway to god-like status as a Pharaoh or a victim of a Pharaoh. Remember, some Pharaohs exploit our coveting habits. This brings us back to page one. Pharaohs can make our lives very luxurious just like the state around the Nile River. Coveting material goods is a sin because we bargain away our souls and bodies, one bruised piece at a time. After each affair or assault, Pharaoh may let us shop: the worse the offense, the grander the compensation. This is the reward of worshiping Pharaoh. If you do not exchange gods, some part of you will eventually die on your Pharaoh's altar, be it your self-esteem or your body. If you are a Pharaoh, you are not doing much better because you are corroding your own soul as you admit to yourself that you are not god-like and only as human as your Lizzy Strata. Coveting can turn the relationship of a Lizzy Strata and a Pharaoh into an emotional-vampire's co-dependency.

The abuse begins again until Lizzy leaves.

Conclusion

Over the last fifty years in travels through the majority of the United States and more than twenty countries, I have known more Lizzy Stratas and Pharaohs than I can count. Both have been male and female, adults and children. Some lived a life-long cycle of abuse like the old lady in the house without water or electricity that I mentioned in the beginning of this book. Five of the women died from domestic violence. Others die a little each day in relationships that are outrageously violent or subtle emotional and financial prisons. I have seen men beat women on the street in broad daylight on public streets in the US and in England. I have met men and women who pimp themselves in wealthy marriages or as public prostitutes. I have heard sermons, coffee house conversations and I read scholarly documents that attempt to normalize domestic violence. If those speakers and scholars have their way, no one needs a Hell for it couldn't be worse than the one that they advocate in this lifetime.

Too many Lizzy Stratas and Pharaohs have been taught a doormat-christianity that does not follow the teachings of Jesus Christ and that enables domestic violence to the point of what is really a form of human sacrifice on a Pharaoh's altar because people are dying unnecessarily.

The Ten Commandments do not condone domestic violence in any form!

Jesus gave an escape clause in Matthew 18:15-18 for people who are victims of domestic violence!

Whatever your reason for picking up this little book, I hope that you will join a movement that has been going on for thousands of years. That movement is the anti-domestic violence movement.

If you are a Lizzy Strata or if you are concerned about one, I hope that this book has helped you rationalize God's love for you. If you are not a believer, I hope that this book helps you galvanize the path away from domestic violence.

If you are a Pharaoh or if you are concerned about one, I hope that this book helps you find that empty, corroded space of broken self-esteem that cannot be filled by being an emotional vampire and abuser. Whatever thrill you feel from punching, bashing, imprisoning and harming your Lizzy Strata is temporary and expensive and it is an addiction like cocaine and as implosive as opioids. You yourself die a little each time you abuse.

The Ten Commandments are a path out of abuse for both Lizzy Strata and Pharaoh. They are a path toward a fulfilled and healthier life.

Join the movement against domestic violence. See the Ten Commandments as the gift of life that they are.

Live! Be loved!

Notes

Notes

Ten Commandments against Abuse: Love without War

www.ingramcontent.com/pod-product-compliance
Lightning Source LLC
Chambersburg PA
CBHW020940090426
42736CB00010B/1212